Dedication

Promises is dedicated to my daughter Nora in appreciation of her kindness and support

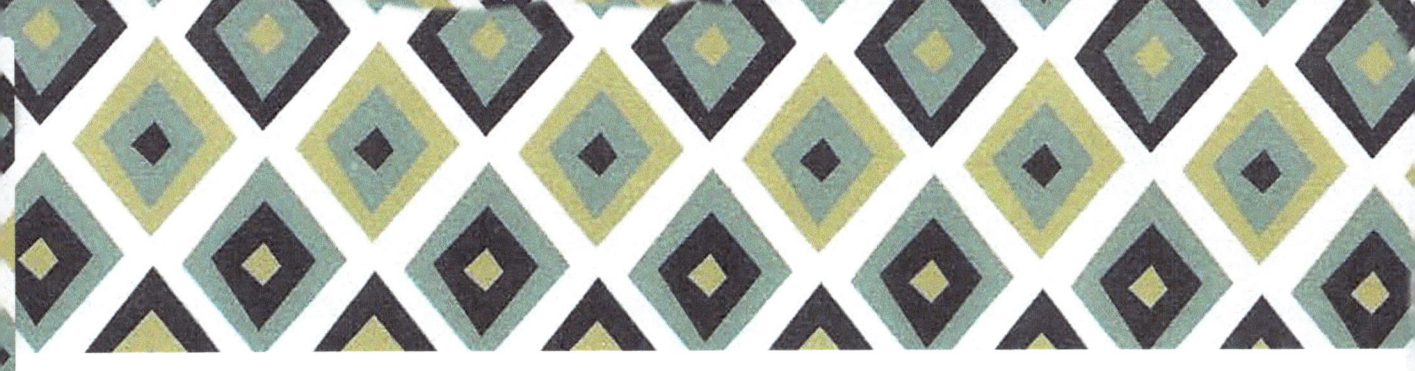

PREFACE

PROMISES is a small book of poems and stories which are mainly focused in the now. Each is accompanied by a painting. All are original works by Barbara Schmitz. The book came into being over a period of two years and was completed in 2022. This was a time of great change both in world events over the course of the pandemic. , and in my life as well. Adapting and growing through change is a theme which weaves through the book. In addition, this little book expresses love of the natural world, an appreciation of beauty, and faith in the spirit within. It is my hope that readers will relate to the challenges of change and take away the caring evident in the pages of Promises.

A number of stories were inspired from "Writers Write", a group of writers who live in Southeast Florida in the Stuart area. A topic may be shared or not, and developed in the way of our choosing. This is fertile ground for creativity. For myself, writing has been a lifelong activity. I have published a number of books which are available on Amazon.

The original works in the book are the property of Barbara Schmitz and may not be copied without the permission of the author.

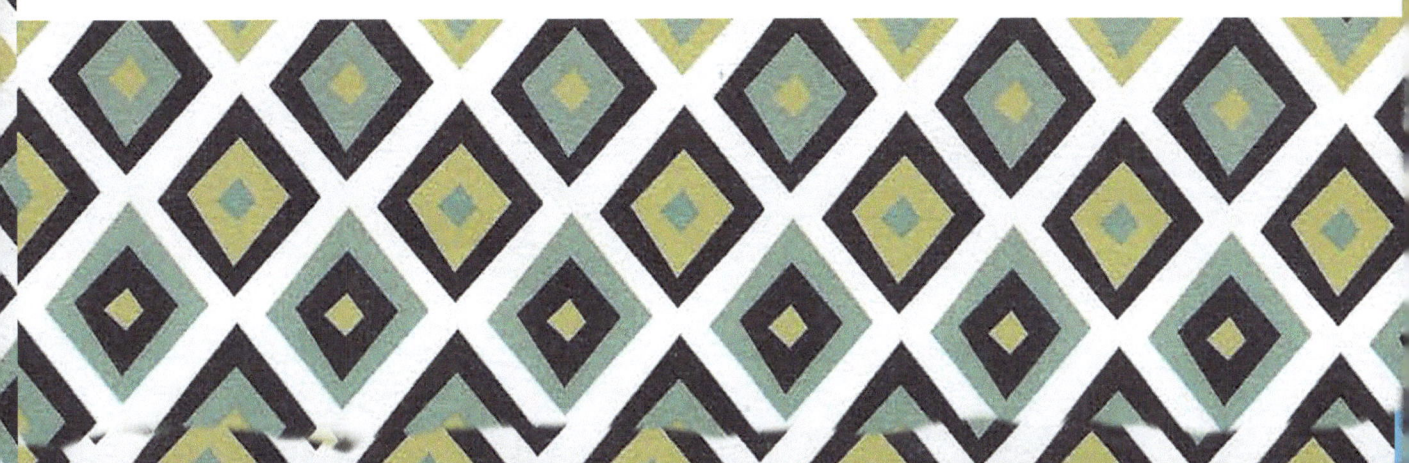

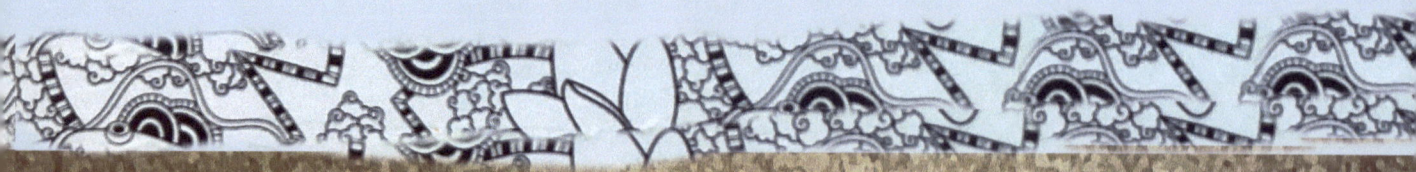

Pussy Willow Surprise

Pearly grey catkins
Low light hides them at stream side
A soft spring surprise
A gleam of reflected light
And the whole day changes

A Tanka by Barbara Schmitz
September 1, 2022

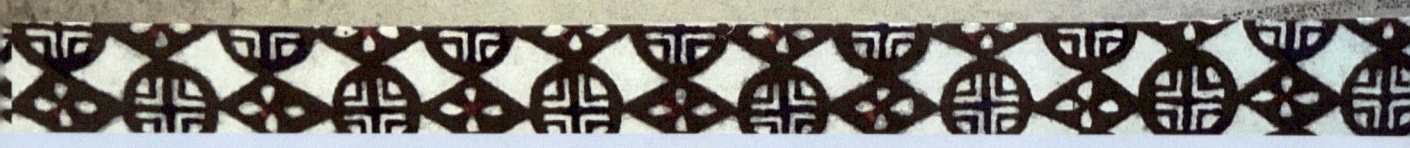

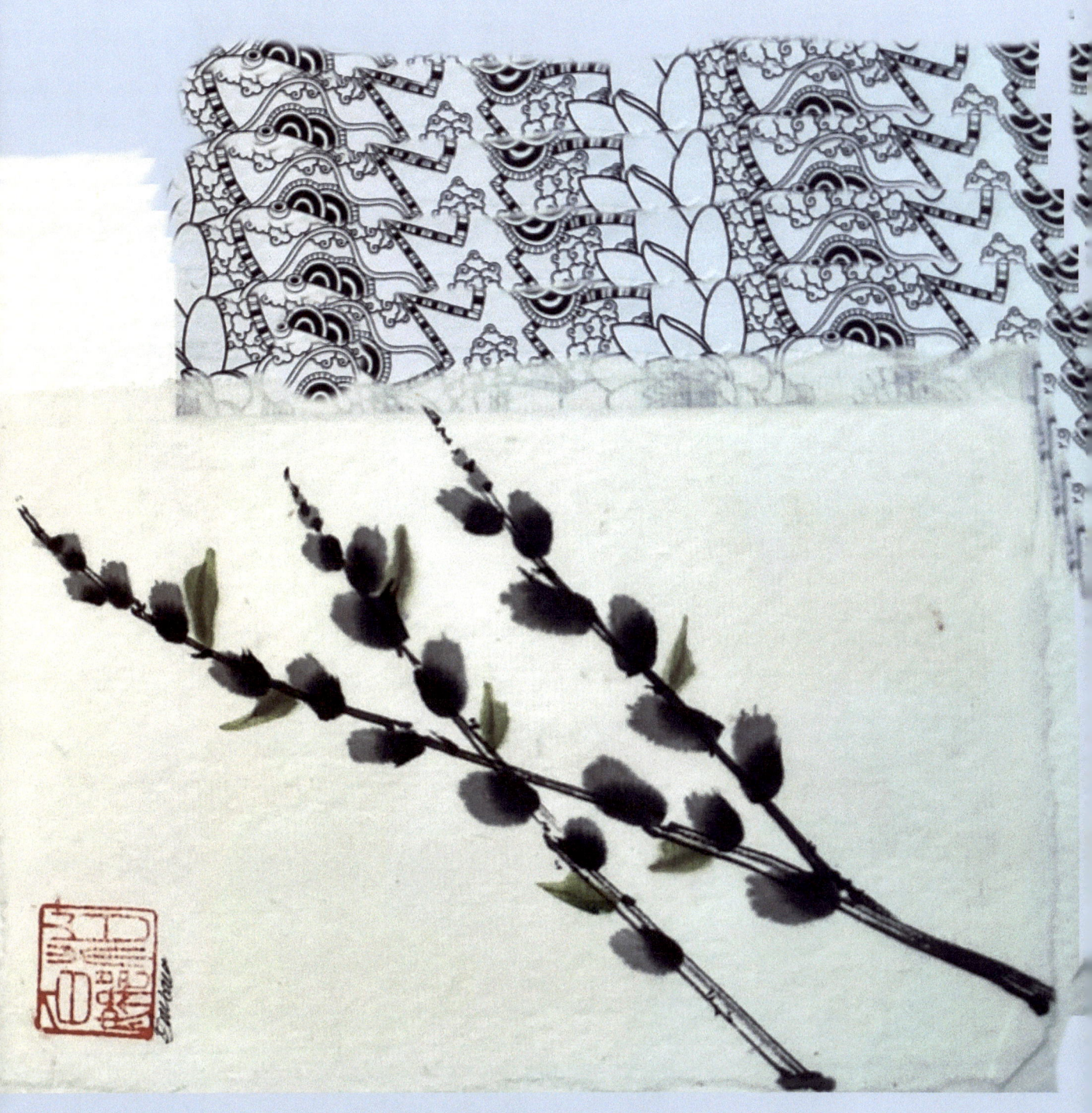

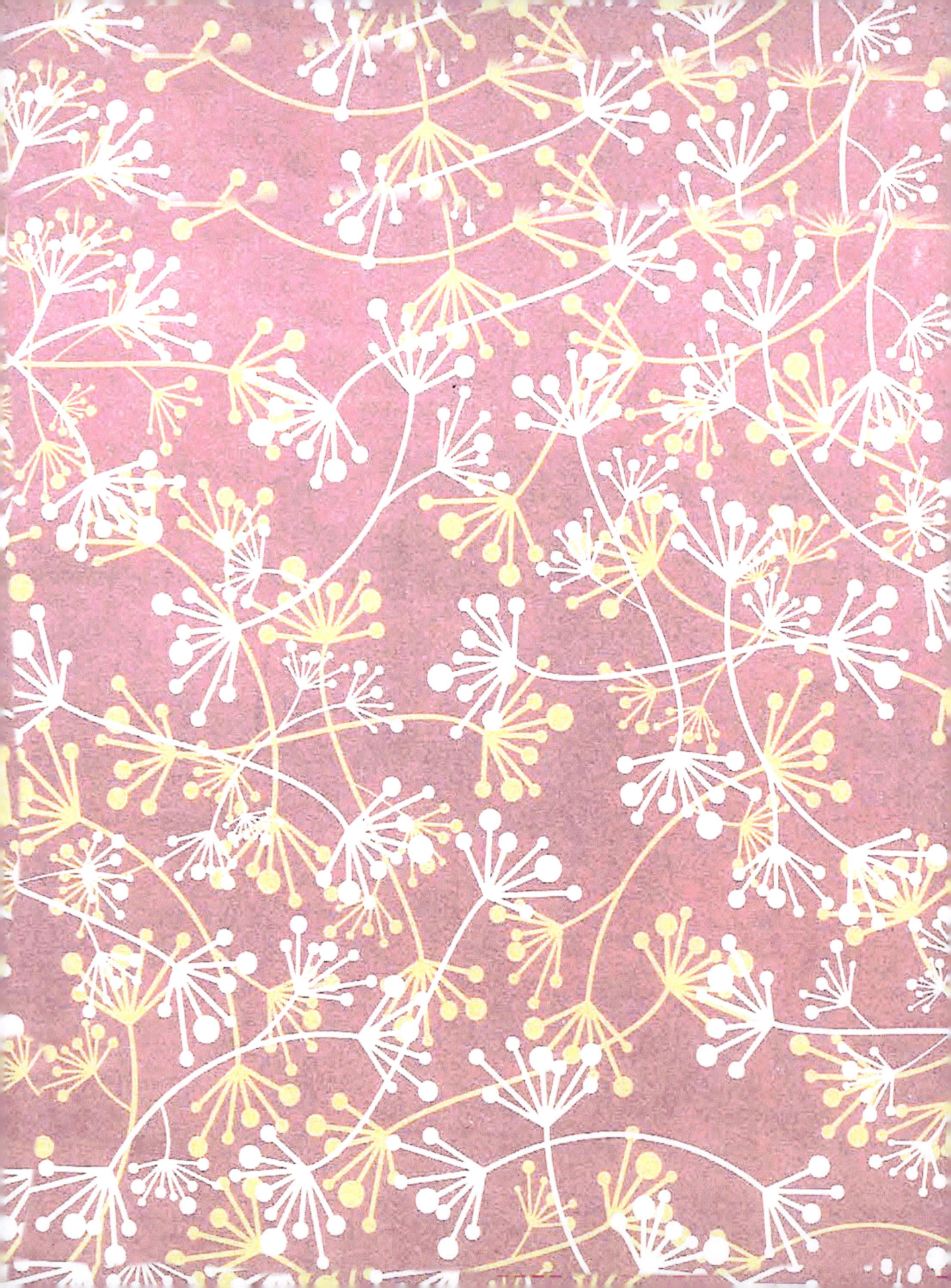

An Old Sweet Song

How does one remember when it's been so long ago
Years have passed since I was small it's been so long ago

In my mind I see them still a solid German couple
They're standing side by side
They greet the son, his wife and children with festive foods
They show with pride

Minnie's kitchen, her ham spread, the breads and
Pies on view waiting
Pork roast and bratworst, and sauerkraut in the air,
All is for the tasting

The midday meal weighs the table as we gather
Where windows show the skyline
Beer for adults, milk for the kids and the food and
More food tastes just fine

So different from our lives back home,
There's the hoosier at one wall
I wonder at the flour bin, at the kitchen, at it all

Adults talk as children stay quietly nearby
They speak of who's married whom, the neighborhood changes
Business my father has tried

Later I'm free to wander Grandpop's greenhouses,
The earth smell, the grapes and the plants
The flower shop with cool cases of blooms
That was made to help out my aunt

Then I'm taken to where I will stay
The room where Aunt Adelaide resides
There on a pink satin quilt a porcelain faced baby doll lies

She's there each time we visit,
Her soft body to handle carefully
Later I wished for the doll to be mine
 But that was never to be

It's a memory woven into my life
As while browsing antiques there came into my sight
A doll in a cradle in somebody's booth
That matched Aunt Adelaide's doll just right

I brought that doll home and fixed what was needed
And researched her history with pleasure
We found her a cradle after looking for months
Where she sleeps near my bed, as a treasure

My quilting friend Rosie had just the right cover
A doll quilt in four square design
Her fingers made it with old timey fabrics
It fits in the cradle just fine

Each time I linger and look at the doll
At the cradle and fabrics and all
I think of Aunt Adelaide, Minnie and Grandpop
And my childhood visits recall

I think, too, of my friend Rosie now gone
My husband who helped the project along
Old times and new, blended together
They sing out a sweet memorable song

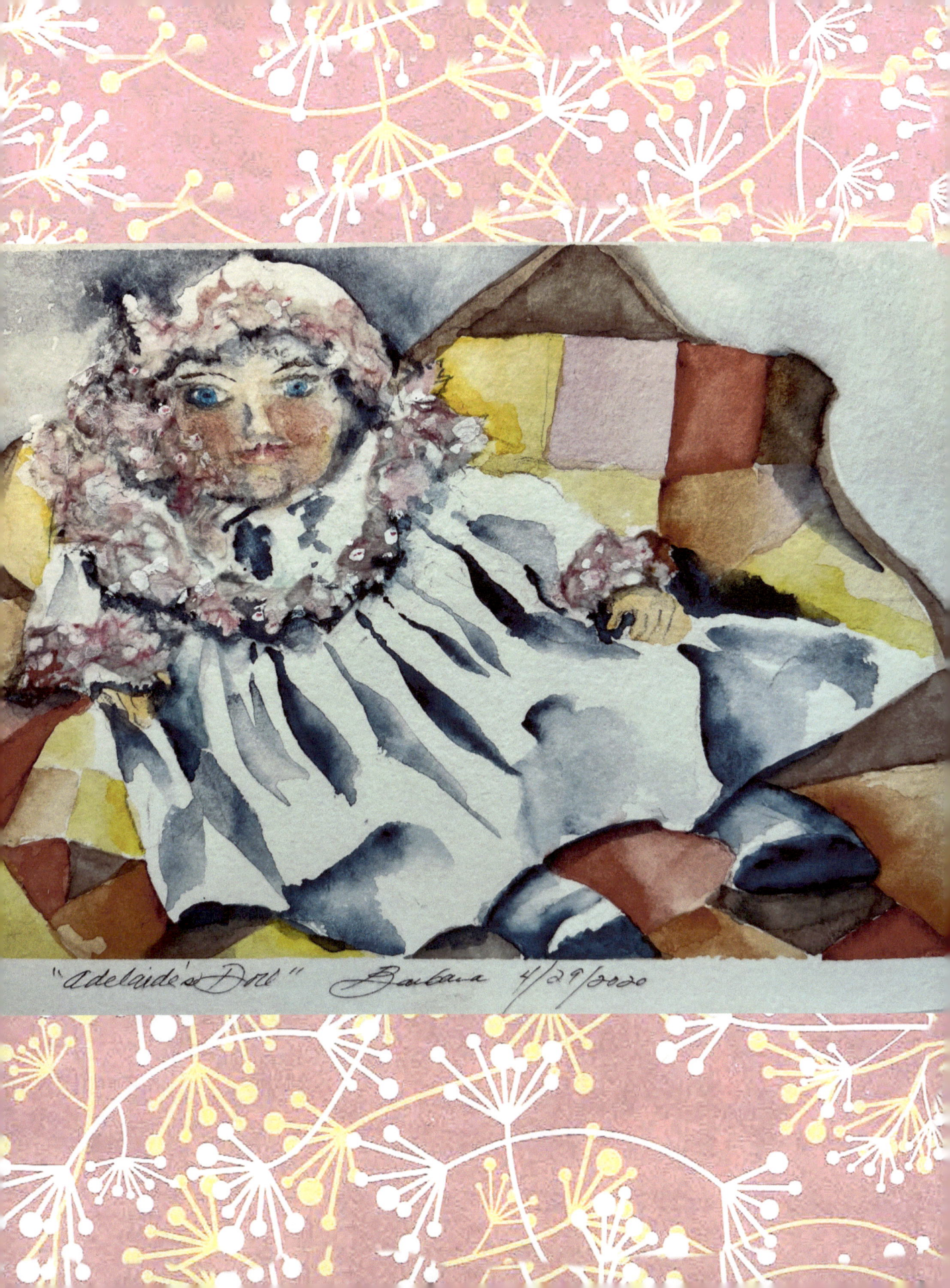

"Adelaide's Doll"   Barbara 4/29/2020

MOTHER'S DAY

I rose this morning
My eyes on an old photo
Three women posing
Mother, Grandmother and me
Precious female lineage

Common heritage
Forward and back the chain grows
Daughters now witness
Creating, building and giving
Working, loving, ripples spread

I grew a violet
Because my mother loved them
I told my daughter
She had planted one as well
Thinking of the joy Mom had

Barbara Schmitz
May 9, 2021

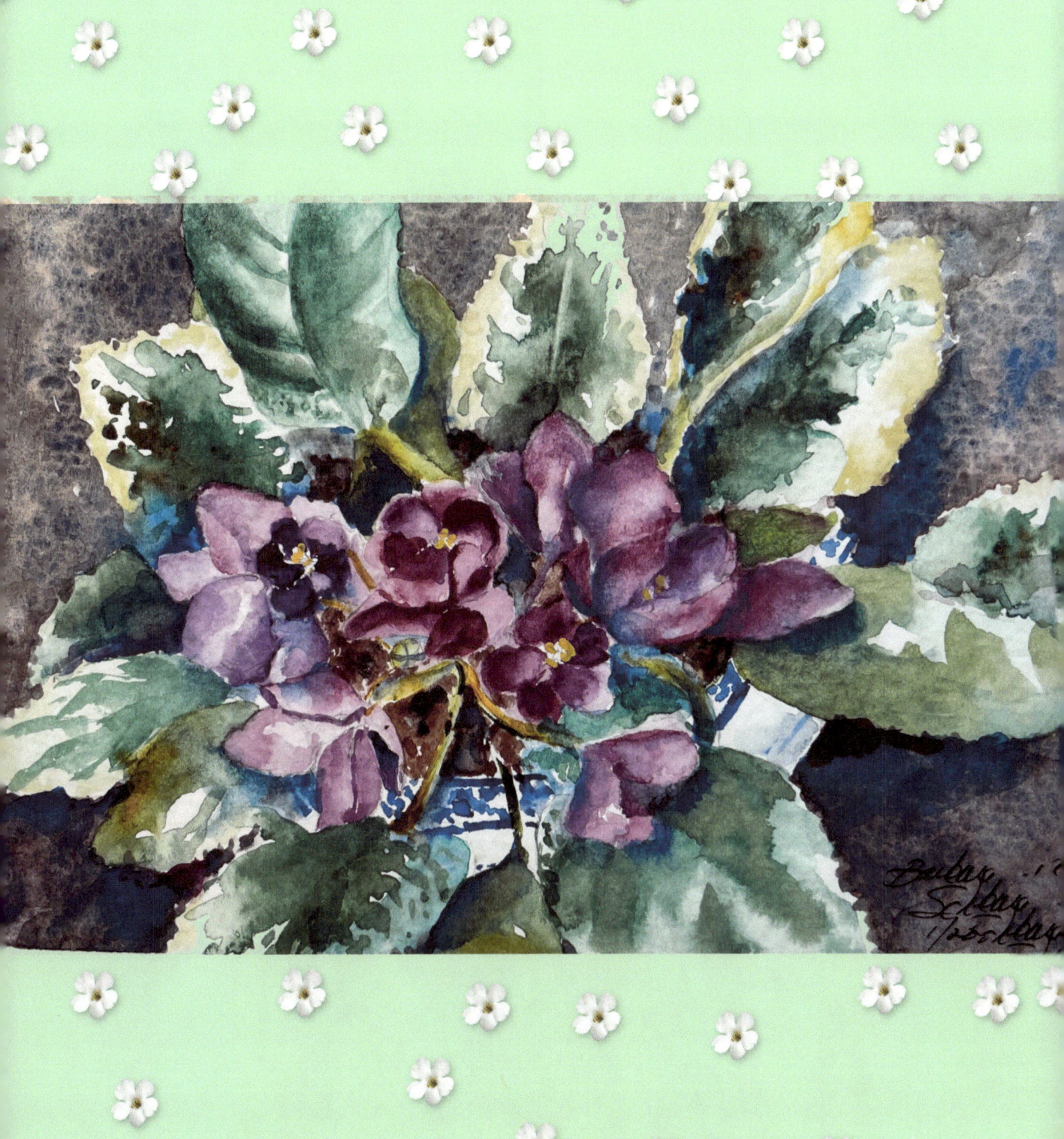

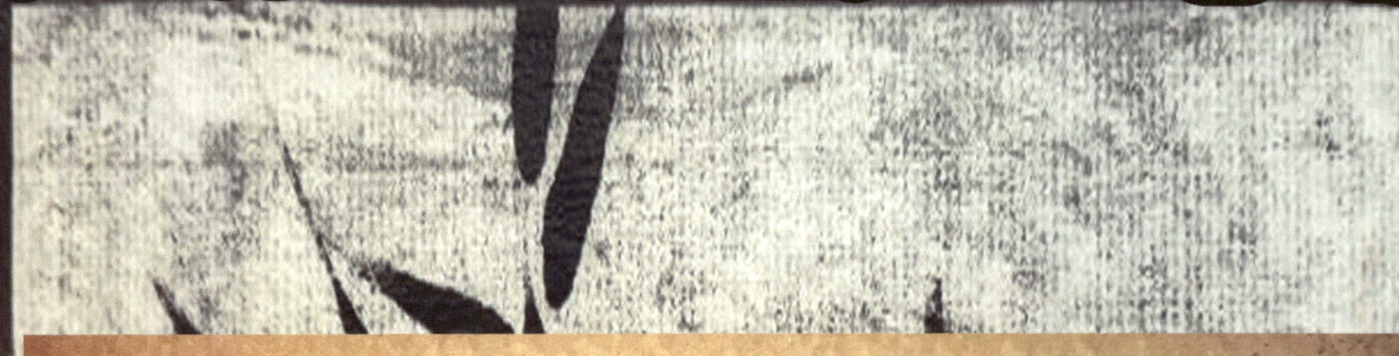

A Day Trip to the McKee Botanical Gardens

A day of exploring, of beauty, art, and friendship, a day of getting away from it all - that was our day at the McKee Botanical Gardens in Vero Beach.   My friends Judy and Tycho and I did the two hour drive to discover what the Gardens had to offer on a pretty Florida spring day in April. Leggos was the attraction. Artist Sean Kenny had created life-size animals solely from leggos! He is a renowned artist and we were treated to his creations in a beautiful way.   As we wandered through the gardens, we saw polar bears, a panther, a gigantic monarch butterfly and more. The zebra in my painting was among these amazing works of art. The animals were incorporated into the magic of the gardens which were full of blooming pond lilies, tall bamboo and other exotic tropicals. We had a tasty lunch later at the cafe in the gardens, then visited the charming gift shop before leaving.   As we talked over our experience on the way home, we agreed that we had made the most of a great spot.

Barbara Schmitz
4/22/21

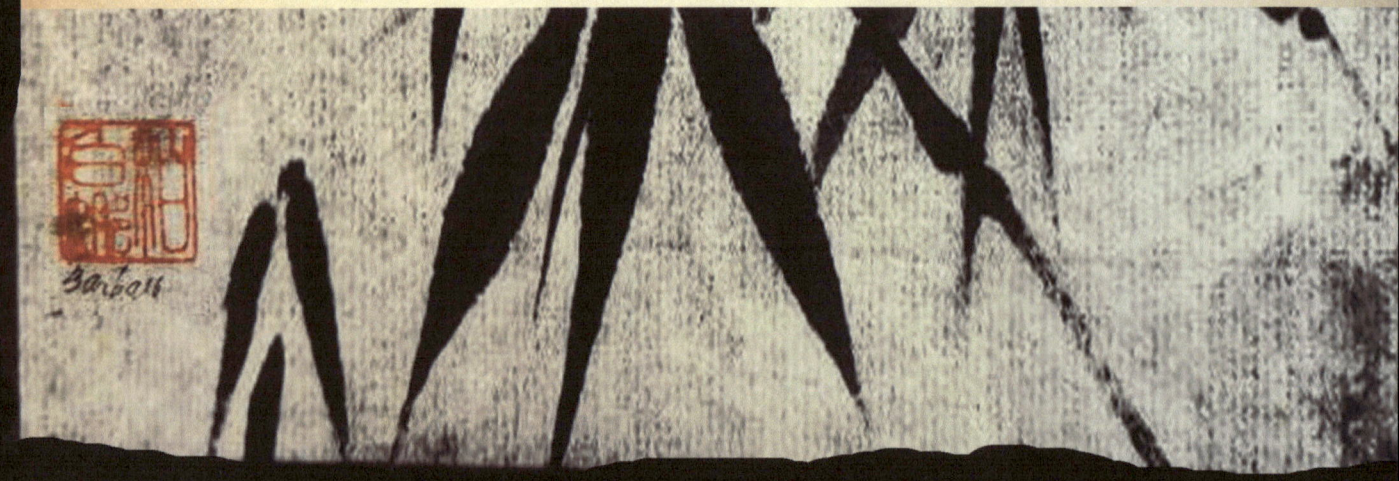

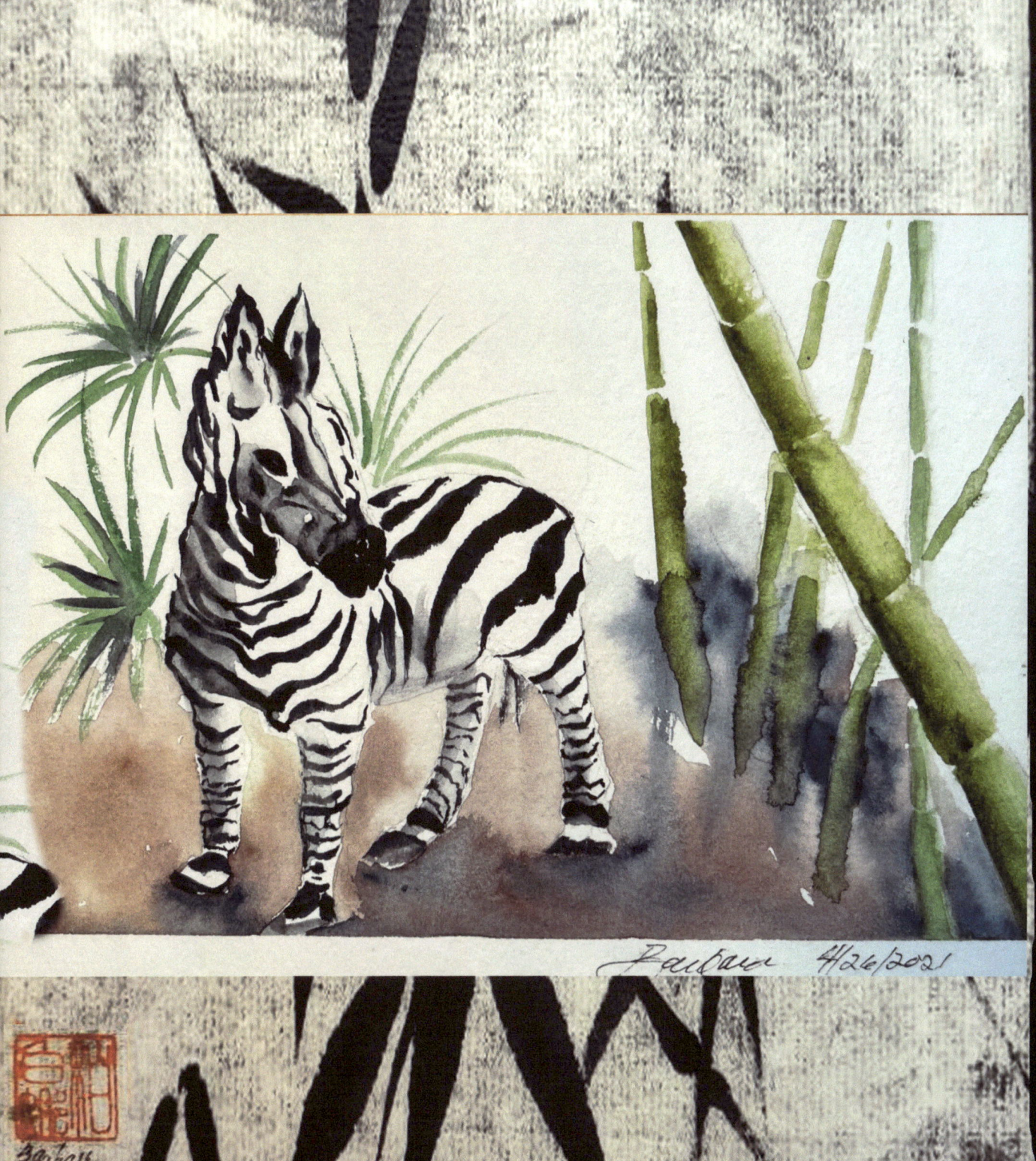

Barbara 4/26/2021

Afternoon at Sandsprit Park

My dog ZuZu and I are going to Sandsprit Park in Port Salerno, Martin County, Florida. I live only 15 minutes away. It's an easy drive along winding SE St Lucie Boulevard leading to Manatee Pocket and the park. I spy boats to my right and head directly in. There are many boat trailers belonging to folks out on the water today. I head toward the water, benches and car parking. I draw in a sharp breath at the sight of the prussian blue of the St Lucie River today and pull in to a good parking space. My eyes sweep the water. There are few white caps visible. The water is almost flattened by an Easterly breeze coming directly from the inlet and off the ocean. It must be an incoming tide. The deeper dark blue mixes with shades of aqua. There are people and boats on the spoil island directly out from us. They are walking in the shallow water on the sandbar. On this mid July day, the spritely breeze is welcome and refreshing. I check my watch which tells me that the temperature is 82 degrees. Just lovely. Amazing. The blue sky is hazed a bit with high blown clouds, so we are somewhat protected from the hot sun.

ZuZu waits patiently while I get out her stroller and attach her bright red leash to her matching halter. I smile, she's so cute. She eagerly walks with me to a bench along the docks. Birds loudly chatter from the seagrape trees overhead. I think I hear parrots but see only black grackles. Pelicans and shorebirds are abundant, flashing white as they skyrocket upward on the air. The breeze does a job with both of us, as our hair blows about our faces. The stroller waits nearby.

Boats are heading into and out of Manatee Pocket at a great rate. There are several large sport fishing boats in shades of blue with tall fly bridges. A large sailboat is being towed on a line by a towboat service. I watch that, wondering about it. A pontoon boat churns by with a tiki bar aboard and passengers celebrating just being alive today, like us. The Island Princess , a large sightseeing craft with two decks hosting onlookers, passes slowly. They're getting their view of the park. We watch them; they watch us. It rounds toward it's mooring spot at the Marriott Hotel, then returns a bit later with another load of passengers. There are many smaller sport craft. It seems like a fast moving parade. Water churns into white wakes from boats whizzing by, the wind always with us.

There are numbers of people about. The couple standing in front of us at the dock greet us and talk about Zuzu and her stroller. They tell of their Yorkie who panics if they put him into their carrier. They give good wishes as they leave. A man nearby plays music on his phone and sings, he's in his own world. Another walks by with his big brown lab. He sports large sneakers and a casual air. Folks near me fuss over his dog and I hear him say he'll be by again on his next lap. Sure enough he's by again and gets fussed over once more. Many people come to Sandsprit Park with their dogs. There's much greeting and sharing of stories about their animals.

We leave our bench to walk the lengthy dock. We pass people fishing, people at tables under pergolas, others in lounges watching the water, or reading. We get a better look into the Manatee Pocket with boatyards and fish houses and many many boats tied into docks. We walk back to sit once again before heading home. I lift Zuzu into her stroller and we walk toward the car. We pass a couple who talk with us while the wife holds their black and brown rat terrier/chihuahua mix in her lap. His name is Max and he brandishes that on his halter. She says she's seen me at the park before and declares Zuzu to be the ultimate cutest dog she's ever met. I smile and nod at that. She says she loves coming to the park, it's so breezy and people are nice. She comes often. I agree. It is breezy and people are nice. I come often too.. In fact it's our favorite Martin County place to be.:.

Barbara Schmitz, July 25, 2021

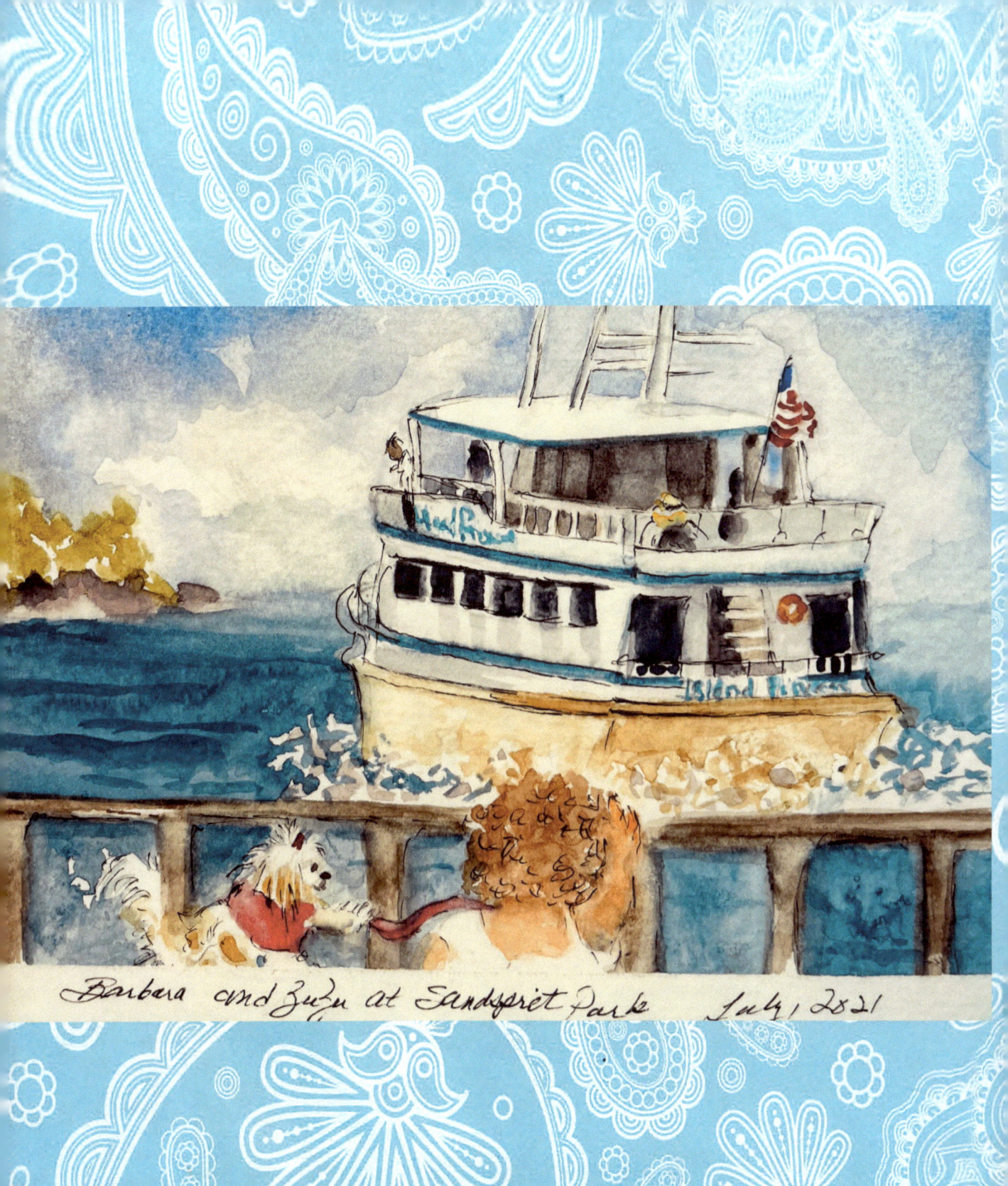

Barbara and Zuzu at Sandspirit Park   July, 2021

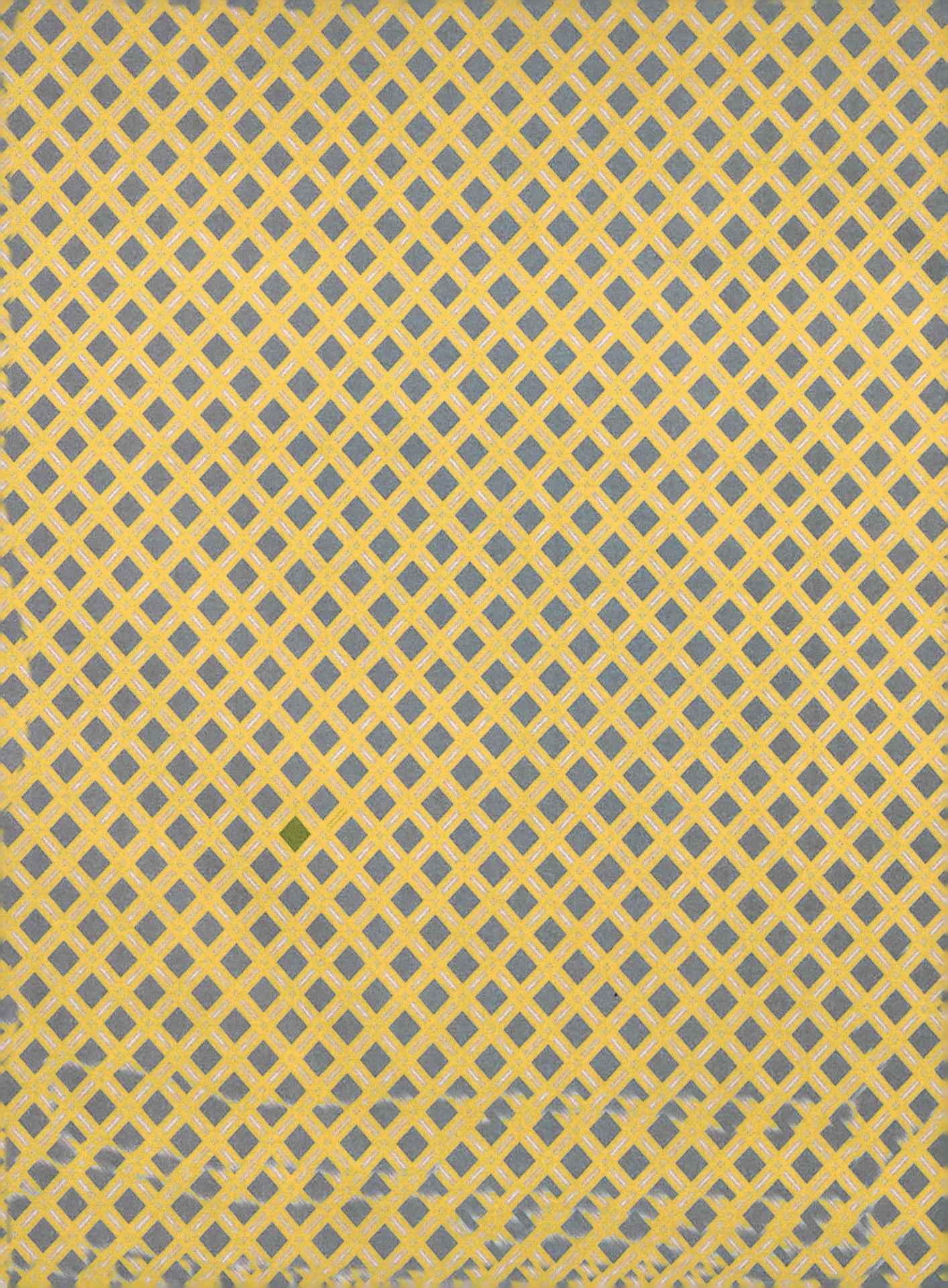

A Conversation With Van Gogh
by Barbara Schmitz 8/21/2021

Vincent said.......If you truly love nature you will find beauty everywhere

I reply......Quiet spellbound witness
Whistling duck pair, wings trembling
Watch and wait for sunrise
Eastern orange glow delivers
A realized anticipation

Vincent said....... Seek only light and freedom and do not immerse yourself
in the worldly mire

I reply.......Pleasant evening
Conversations all around
Dining together
While across the darkening river
Rises a full golden moon

Vincent said......Art is to console those who are broken by life

I reply.......Thinking and dreaming
A ripening of spirit
An idea is born
All else outside disappears
Now just Intense joyous energy

Vincent said......I have nature and art and poetry, and if that is not enough,
what is enough?

I reply......A lifting of soul
Communes with trees air water
Life force within these
An expression from my heart
Feeling just now fully whole

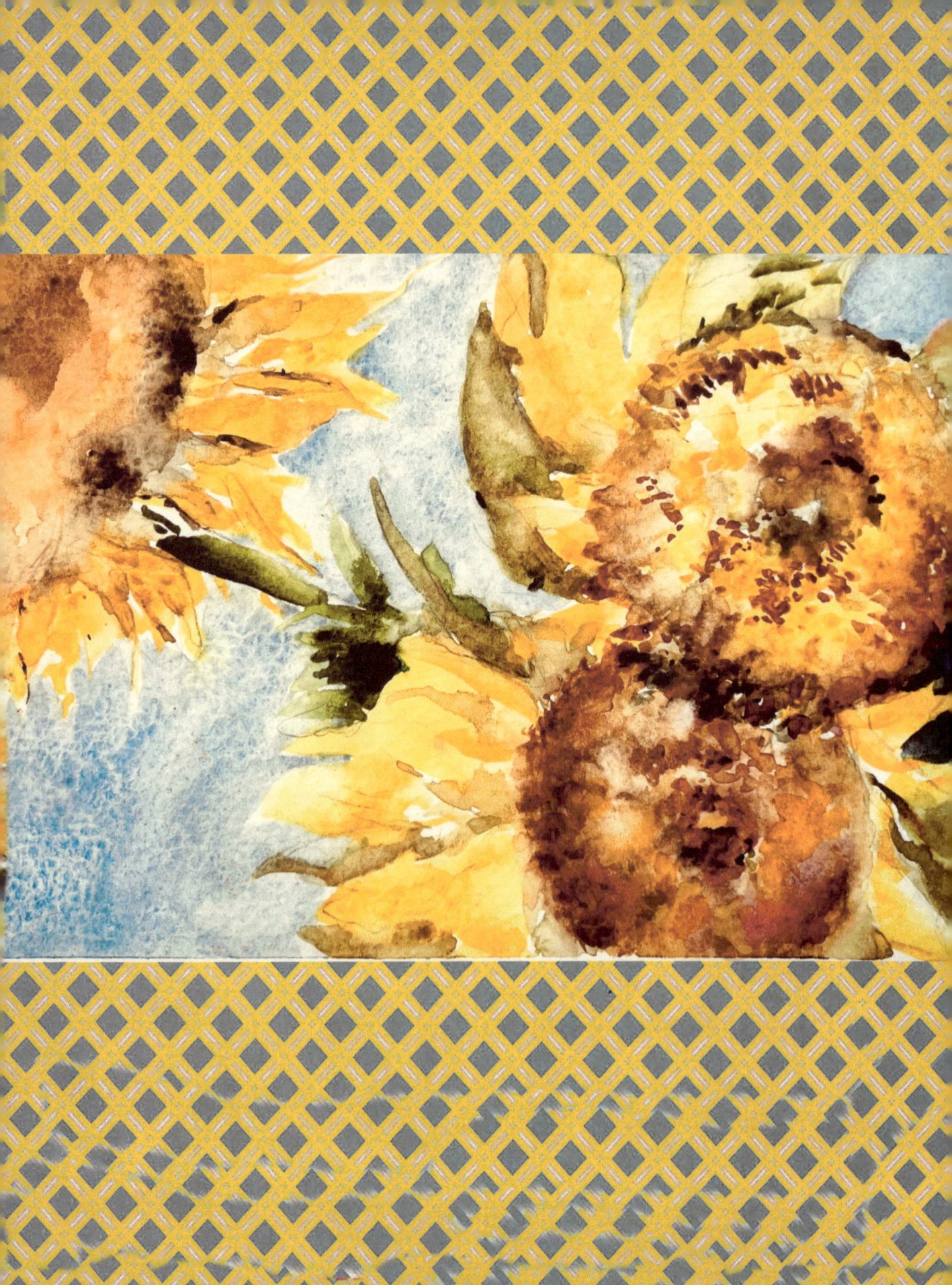

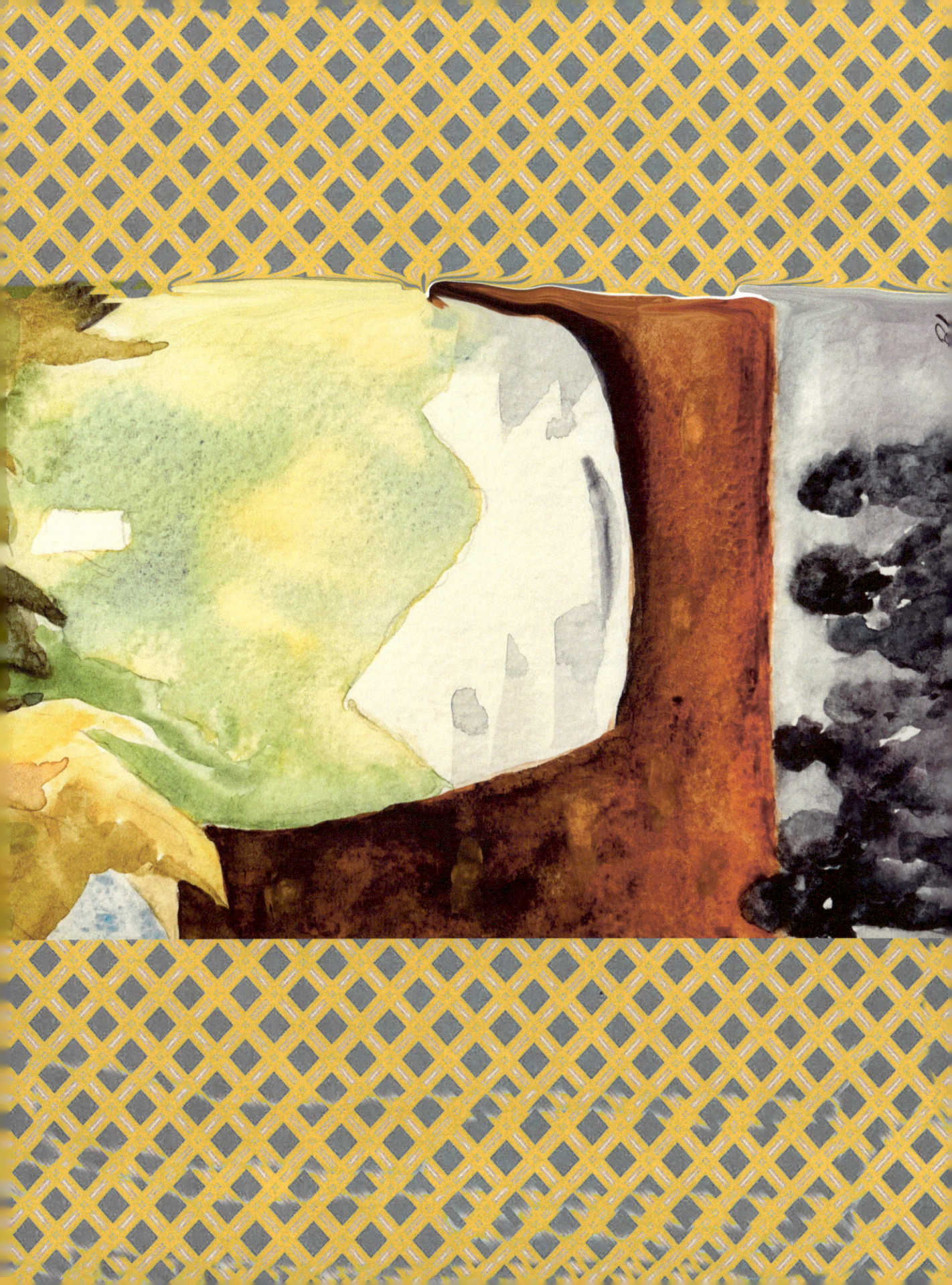

Tree Swallows

Tree swallows swing through the air
Soaring with energy, speed and grace
Wings outspread, shining white breasts
Backs and wings an iridescent Prussian blue
Numbers fly over the lake out back
Then swirl down to sparkling water
Catching air currents over treetops and down the lanes
I see them everywhere, even at the local grocers!

I've been watching for signs of autumn
Checking the papers for temperatures up north
Will the late August sun give a golden light
Will it be time to plant some lettuce
Will it be dark when I awaken
Will September heat subside
My answers come with the tree swallows
Their joyous appearance is the sign
They're here from the north to winter over
My heart lifts and soars with them in celebration

Barbara Schmitz; September, 2021

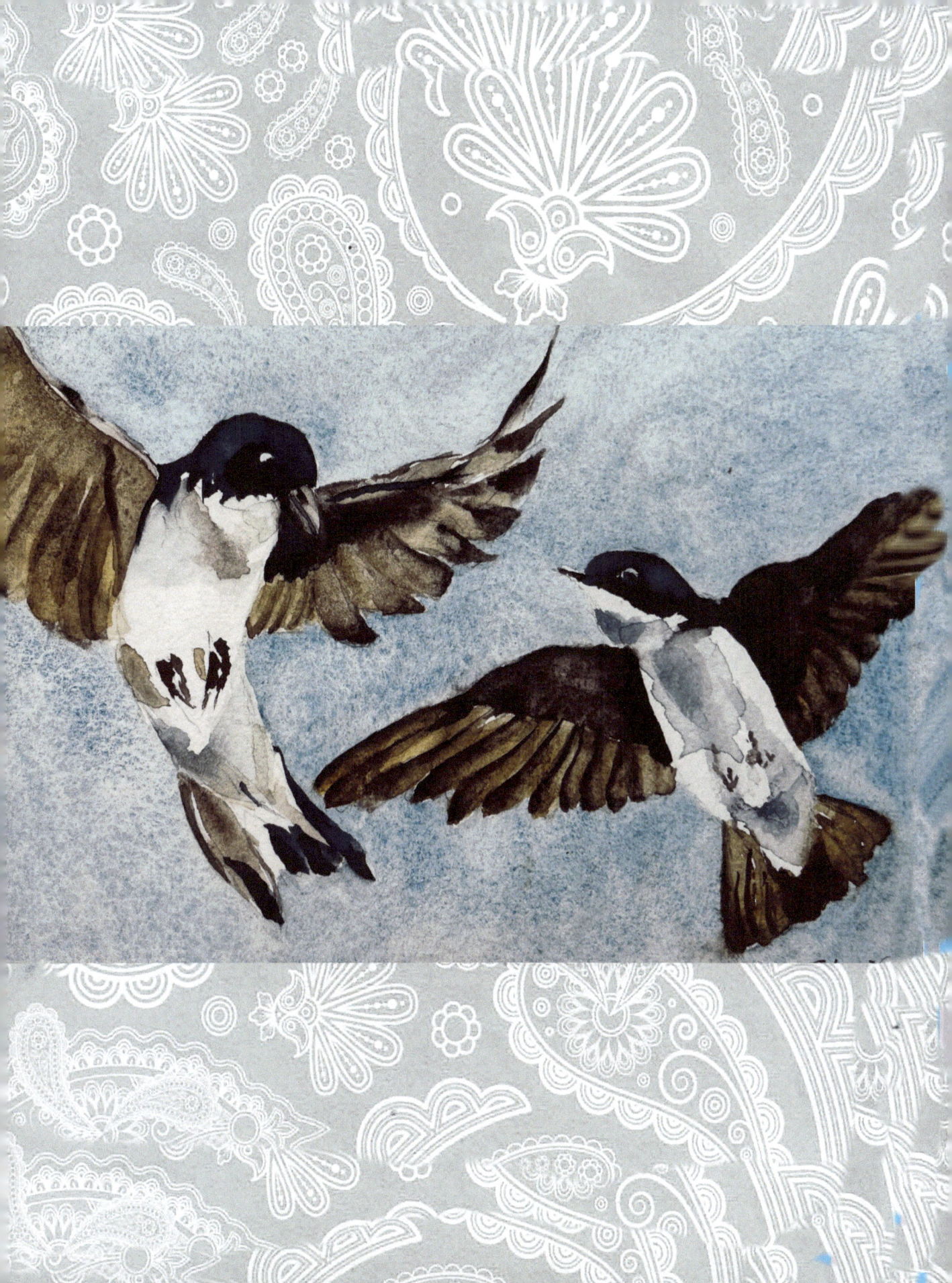

LOVE IS

A FORCE

OVERWHELMING

EXISTING EVERYWHERE

SPIRITUAL BINDING

STRONG

MYSTERIOUS

REAL

THE GLUE THAT HOLDS THE WORLD TOGETHER

ONLY BREATHE AND BE AWARE

IT IS THERE

ENDLESSLY AVAILABLE

BEFORE BIRTH

AFTER DEATH

ALWAYS

Barbara 2/2022

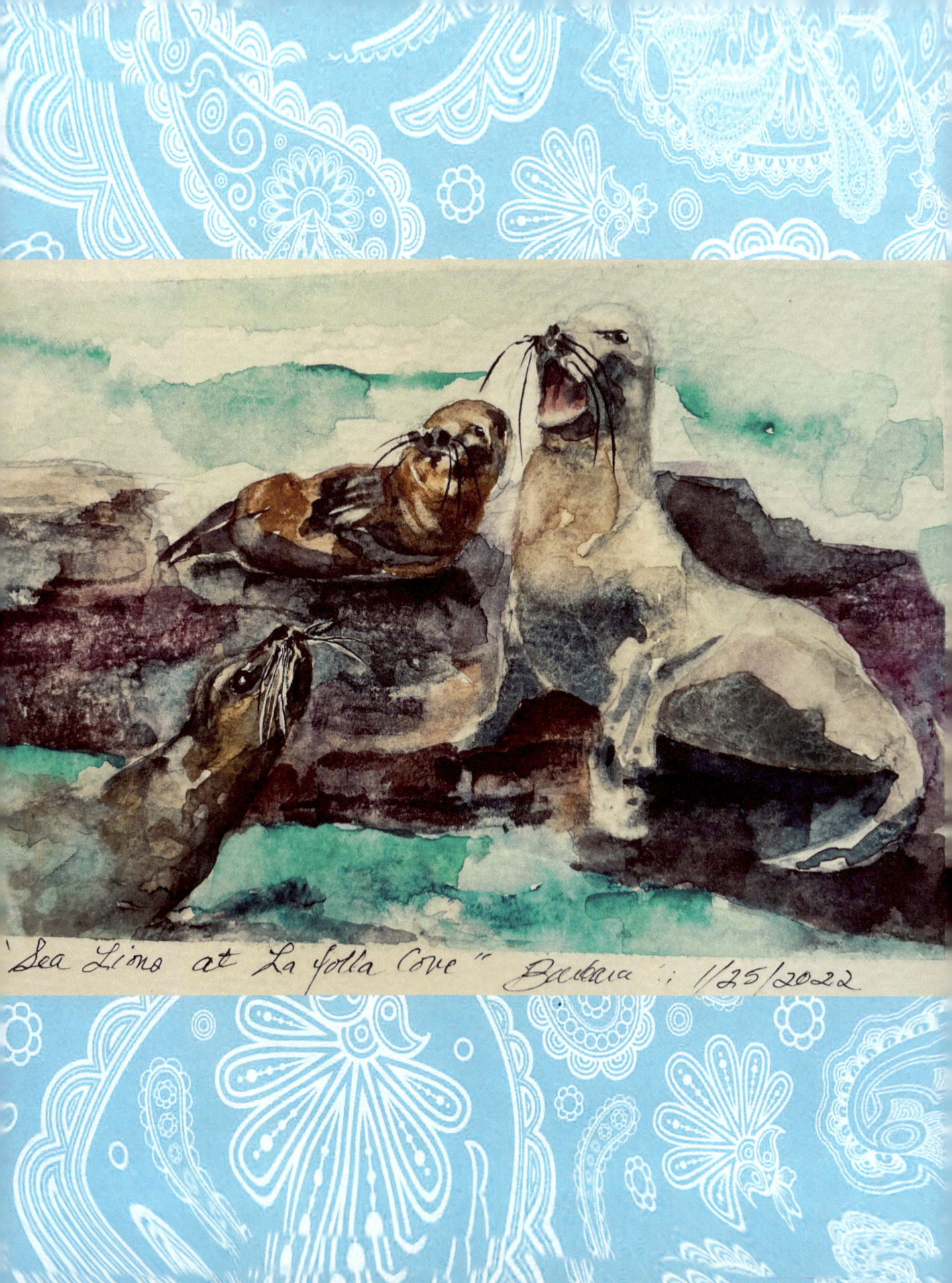

"Sea Lions at La Jolla Cove"   Barbara : 1/25/2022

Thoughts of you

In Tanakas.   By Barbara Schmitz. Jan 18, 2022

Thoughts of all of you
Persist in my mind these days
Essence of your words
Telling of new born attempts
To create, to hope and dream

Efforts of waking
Of seeing the light once more
Lessen confusion
Blankets of foggy layers
Beginning to peel away

What's left of us now
Is not the same as once was
but there's burning light
To illuminate the change
and to celebrate our souls

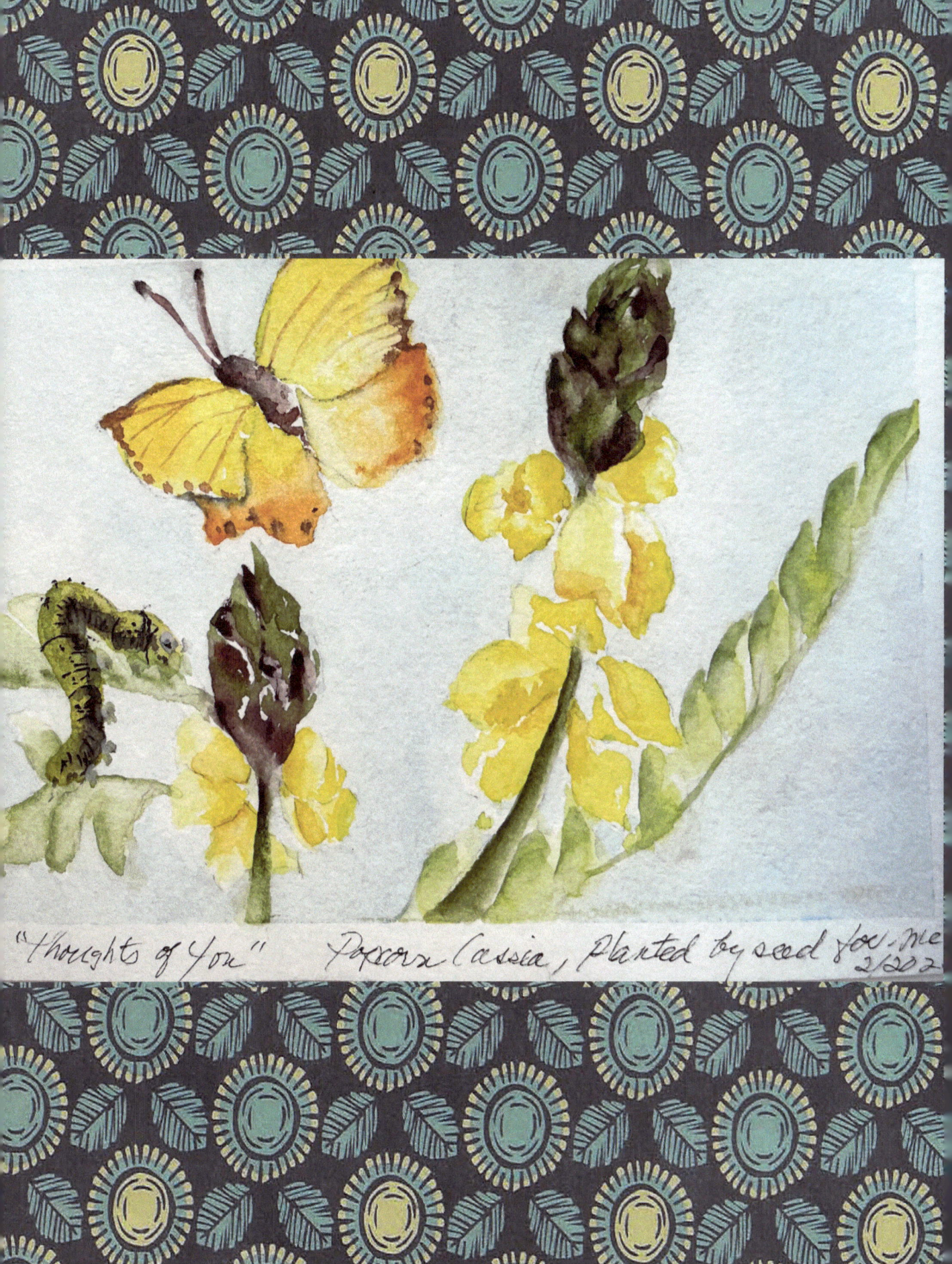

"Thoughts of You"   Popcorn Cassia, Planted by seed for me
2/202

Becoming

Buddha says what you think you become
I think of a day in Cloudcroft New Mexico
When deep rolling hills beguiled me
Into an illusion of isolation
Then the eerie bagpipe sounded
Echos of lonely melody in a single strand
Threaded its way into my heart
And I became the song

I think of the Atlantic Virginia vegetable garden
Where the front several rows were planted with seeds
Of zinnia, cosmos and sunflowers
That grew so much higher than me
And tempted the butterflies and bees from the meadow
To ravish the flowers in clouds of celebration
As they gorged themselves on the abundant nectar
And I became the garden

I think of the lake at Legacy Cove
Resting, my eyes lingered over water
When at dusk a sudden flock of ibis flew low to the surface
Sounds of wind in a sudden rush of air
They leaned north in one body
Mysteriously black and fast
Disappearing from my view
And I became their spirit

I think of a beautiful Lotus
Symbol of my highest center
Drawing its energy into my body
My chest expands to contain all there is
Exhaling I shift awareness and think of my heart
Spreading what I've created
In love to all
Buddha says what you think you become

By Barbara Schmitz, February 2022

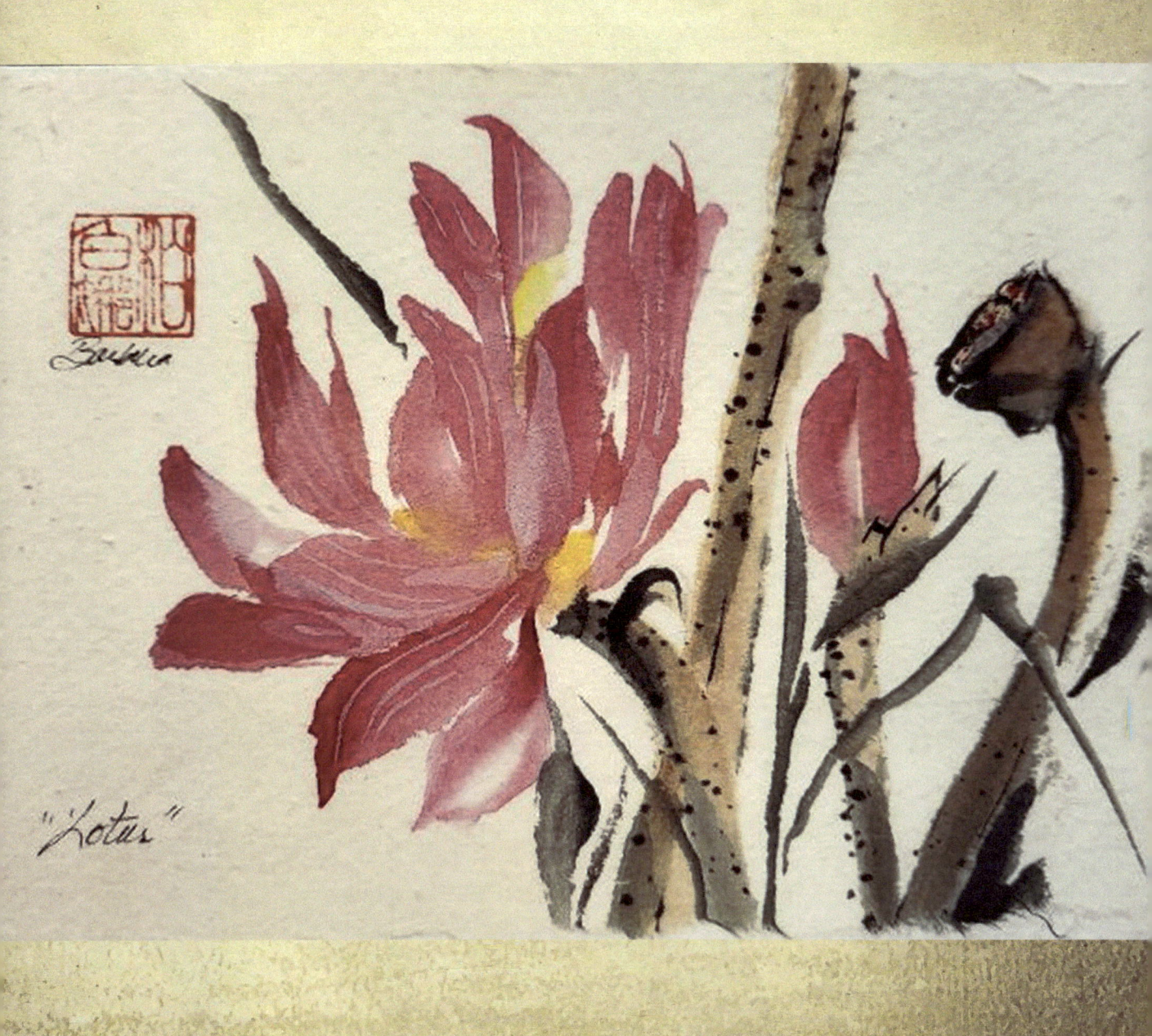

"Lotus"

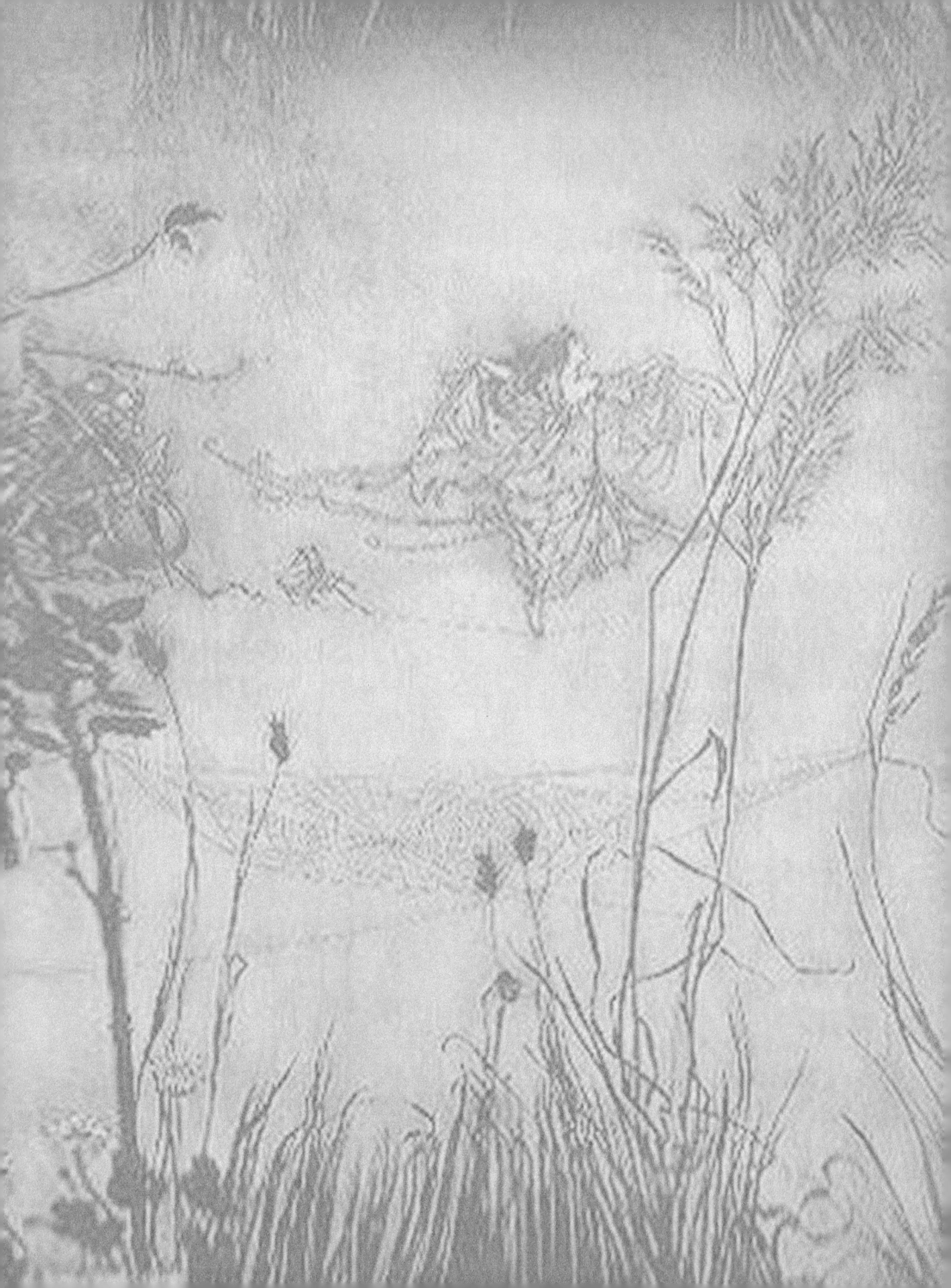

What's in a Name?

It's been decided, a puppy is coming, and soon. My life and hers will change. Some sadness, fear, and loneliness in a time of illness and even death will be lifted. A new friend is about to arrive at my door, hand delivered from far away Missouri.

This little white Shih tzu with golden tan ears and spots needs a name I give to her, not Sisley, what she's been called for the last five months. I need to think of an appropriate name, one with a Chinese flair. The breed was developed many hundreds of years ago in China and was loved by the aristocracy. They are called "Little Lions". An artist friend suggests finding the name of an oriental princess. What a good idea. I spent time online searching oriental princesses. I found numerous other lists of names as well, trying some on my tongue, calling and listening to the sounds. I asked opinions from some of my friends. There is a princess of a thousand years ago who loved poetry, sang and danced and was much loved. Her name ShiShi sounded good. It slid on my tongue, and seemed musical. I thought I'd found it. I later looked up the meaning of the word ShiShi and was chagrined to find it meant "wee wee", and was commonly used in China, especially for children. Oh No! ShiShi wouldn't do! Now what?

I really wasn't inspired by anything and in disappointment went to bed. I had little time left before my new friend was to arrive. Head on the pillow, I let thoughts go, and went to sleep. I was roused in the wee hours. The word "ZuZu" was ringing in my brain. I said out loud, "That's it, that's it! ZuZu is her name!" I remembered the child in the Christmas movie "It's a Wonderful Life" whose teacher gave her a rose. She said, "My teacher says that whenever you hear a bell ring, an angel gets it's wings." Her name was ZuZu. I felt wings around me and was aware of my daughter Suzette's spirit. I knew the name had come from her. Relieved and feeling happy, I went back to sleep.

The next day I looked up the meaning of ZuZu online. There I learned that in Chinese, ZuZu means "Little Pearl". I learned that it's used in several cultures, and is related to any form of the name Susan. I knew that a miracle had occurred during the night. What Suzette had sent to me was just right. Whenever I think of the event of her naming, I'm connected to my daughter as well. Zuzu's full name is, "ZuZu, Little Pearl of Illusion Isle Way".

By Barbara Schmitz, July 4, 2020
Stuart, Florida

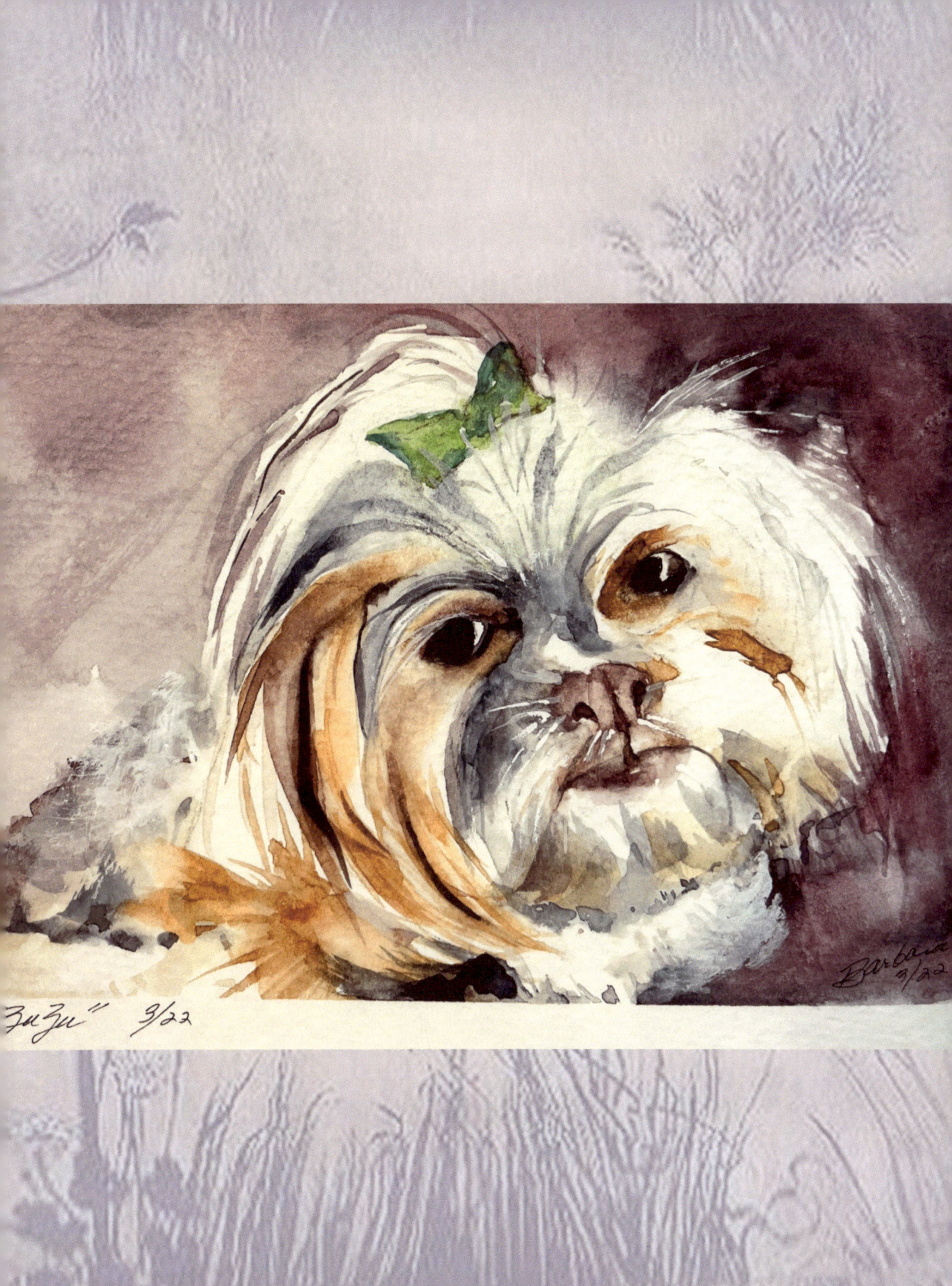

ZuZu" 9/22

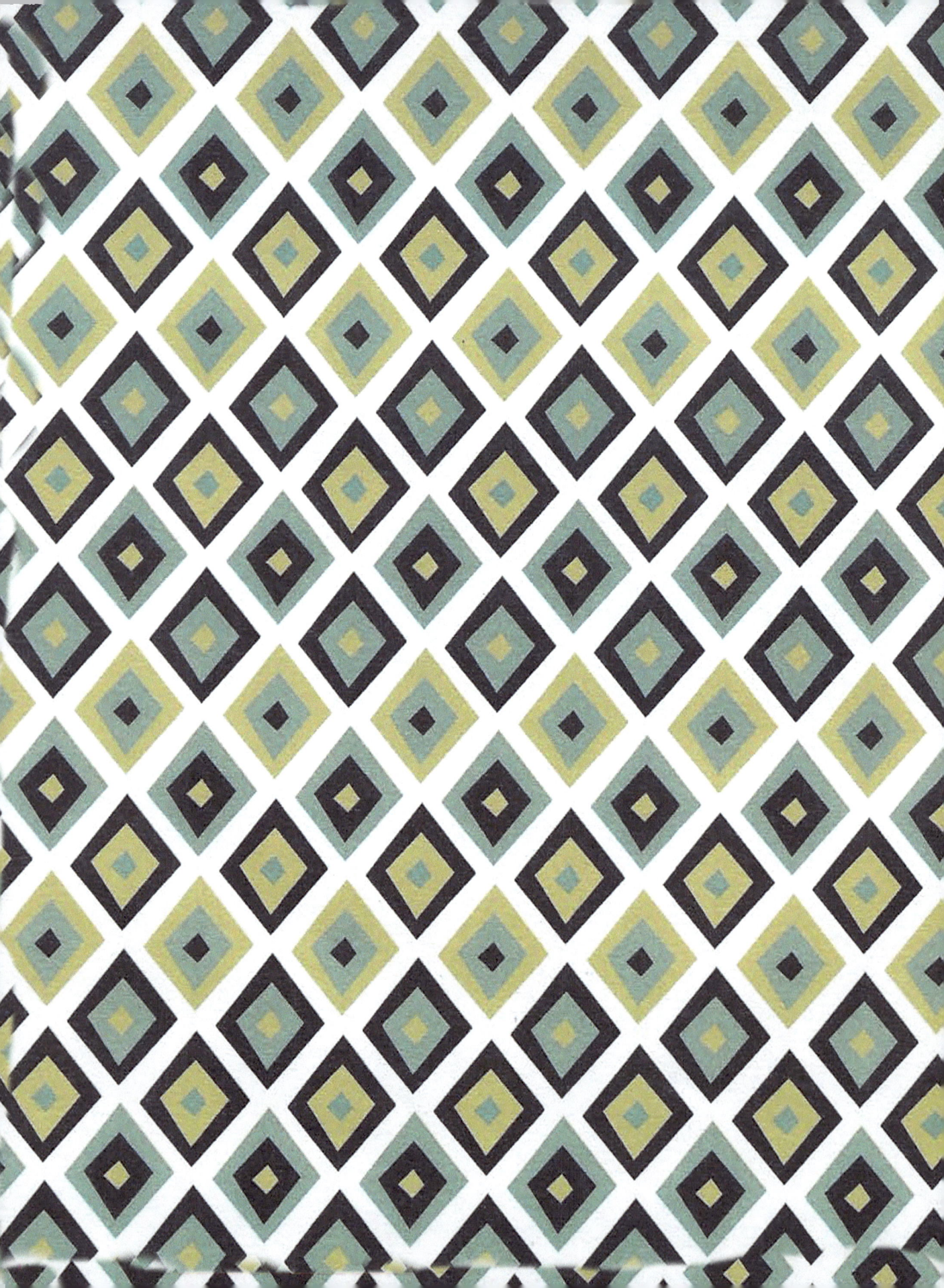

Queenly Affairs

I first met Grace Wakefield when I stopped into her interesting little shop called Tom Thumb on the Eastern Shore of Virginia. Fronting on the busy Route 13 highway, it was an unassuming white old Eastern Shore home with a sign naming it Tom Thumb. It announced garden and craft supplies. I had just retired and was exploring. Gardens and crafts sparked my interest. Inside I found dried flowers and oddities just perfect for browsing. There were publications describing how tos of all varieties. I picked out some unusual flowers for a wreath I had in progress, and struck up a conversation with the proprietor, a charming older woman who after learning I too loved gardens, invited me to see the one at Tom Thumb. Pleased, I said I would indeed like to see her garden. . A small weather worn pavilion served as the entry. We wandered the beds together, watched the busy chickens pecking about the beds. That day she told me the first tale of the many years of stories we would share together. I believe it was a tale of the wayward chickens. One day I called her excited about seeing gold finches swinging on long stems of purple verbena flowers which grew along my fence line. She told me to write a poem about it. I did and that was the start of my journals.

I learned that Grace had joined the Eastern Shore Art League. So she was an artist too! We were off to a great start. Soon we were sharing rides to art meetings and to our monthly paint outs where friendships were formed with many interesting Eastern Shore folks. We got lost in conversation and lost on the winding roads of the shore. At Paint Outs we artists painted together, consumed wonderful pot luck meals at midday and shared ideas and laughter. We would return home weather worn and exhilarated, carrying a new attempt at some piece of artwork. Our abilities grew in that rich soil. One day at an art league board meeting, a conversation about faeries occurred, no doubt due to the huge papier mache fairy hanging above our table which had been created by our hostess and her partner. Grace invited those at the meeting to the Tom Thumb to expand this topic. After all, she was raised in India and England where little people and faeries are held in great respect. "If you want, bring some of your writing along to read," she said.

Grace lined the walls of our meeting room with fairy teapots and other magical items of faeries and buddhas. I brought the poem of the finches. Another brought a family tale of an old hat she wore. This was a magic day of reading our writings, talking about faeries, about ourselves, and making plans. We became the Faerie Writing Group. We decided to continue to meet with the purpose of writing and enjoyment of one another. For over ten years and continuing, we met most months of the year for a day. We were at one another's homes, luxuriating in the time we gave ourselves, staying for lunch, reading our writings and giving ideas. We brought the magic of faeries to our meetings, being silly, dancing, even making faerie wings. The group was kept small and there were no rules. Members changed with life events over time but with much joy and appreciation for one another. The problems which occurred were treated with willingness to work things out.

One day, Grace asked us if Meggie,, her thirteen year old granddaughter, might attend a meeting of the faeries. We welcomed her. From that meeting on, Meggie became a faerie. She went to college, became a lawyer, went to India to work with women's groups, became an organic farmer, went to Ireland and met Eddie, a sympathetic man whom she married. She now has the Irish name of McMullen. She never gave up being one of the faeries. On occasion she would be with us for a meeting and share her writing. She remained always close to Grace and her ideas. The latest magical event is her pregnancy. She will have a baby girl in June whose name is Oonagh Gem McMullen. Oonagh means "Queen of the Faeries", and GEM is a family name of endearment for Grace. Long live our Queen and may as yet unborn Oonagh thrive , live long and be well loved.

By Barbara Schmitz, April 5, 2022

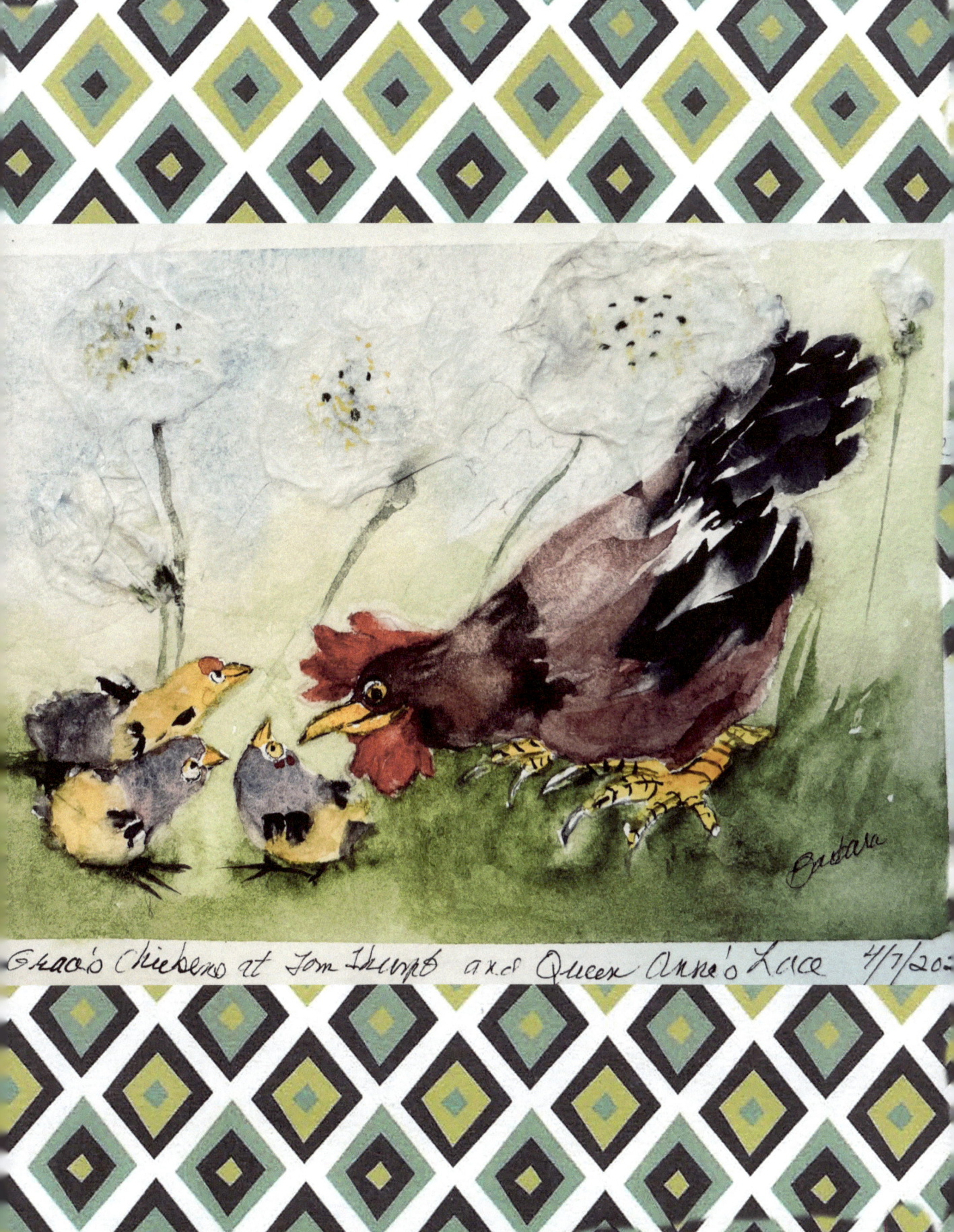

Gracie's Chickens at Tom Thumb and Queen Anne's Lace 4/7/20

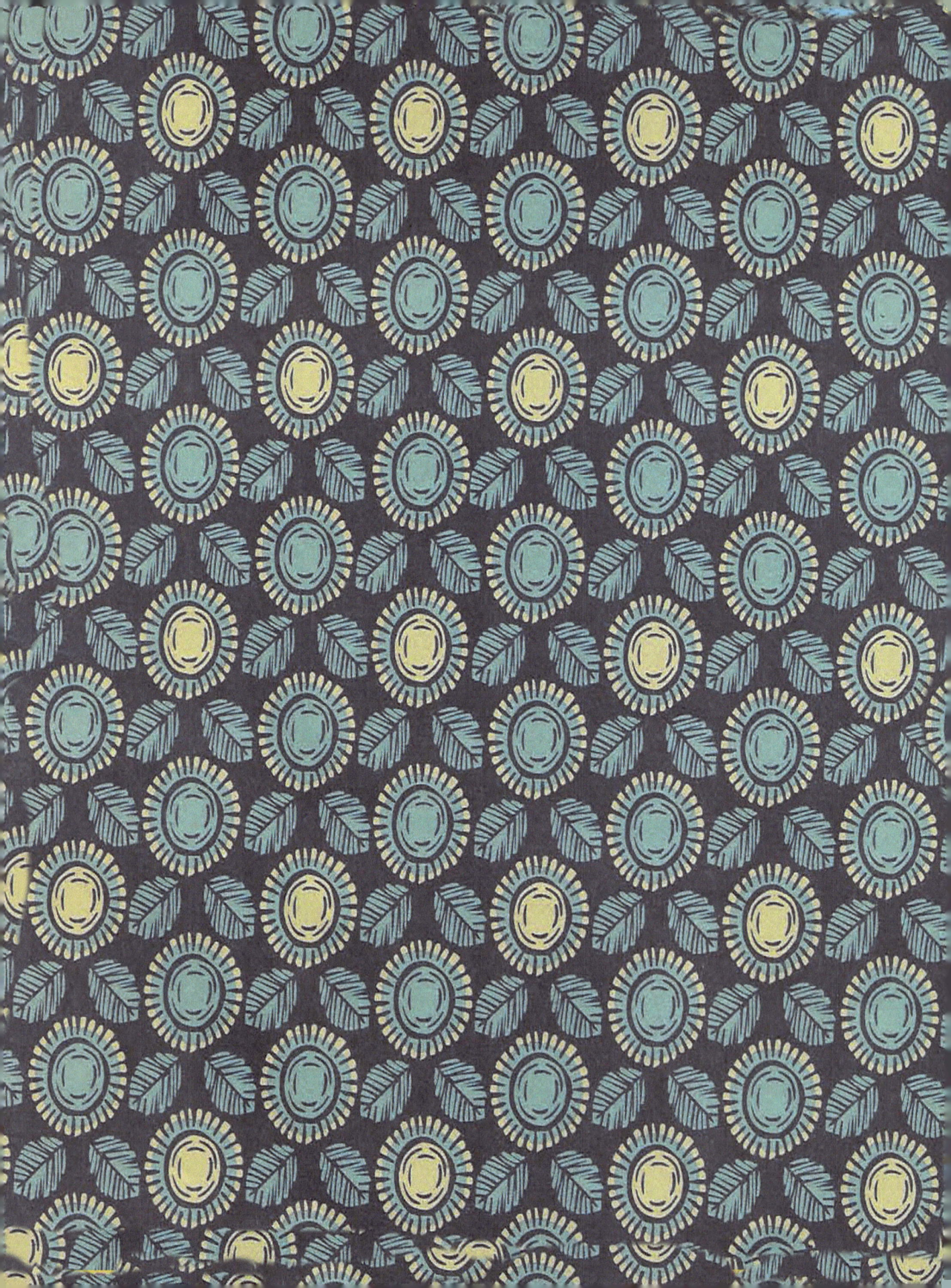

Resilience

I've been riding the energy that flows in and around me
Throughout the universe and beyond
I've been absorbing the stream of love
As it expresses beyond my realization

Out of balance and engulfed in the pounding waves of life change
Tumbling in the rough surf of unknowns and leaving
Heart pounding, elbows and knees scraped
With the sharp edges of daily challenge

There were hands to hold me and ears to listen to the fear
Silent communication in the stillness of early dawn
My needs filled even out of my awareness
Bringing me to another way

So that now I feel the laughter bubbling up inside
As I come to that grassy field where we can meet together
Where possibilities reveal without words
Calling me on

I know in this time there are so many
Who, living in some dark place are overcoming massive injury
May they have our friendly hands and loving healing energy
To help them in their journey

Barbara Schmitz.   May 16, 2022

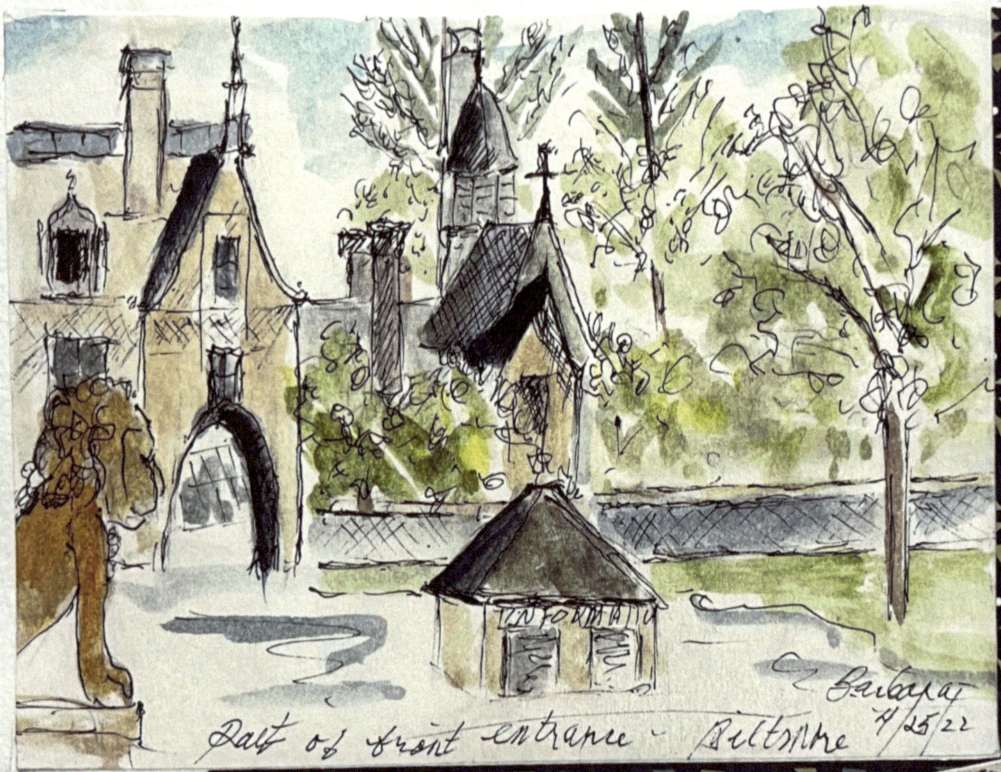

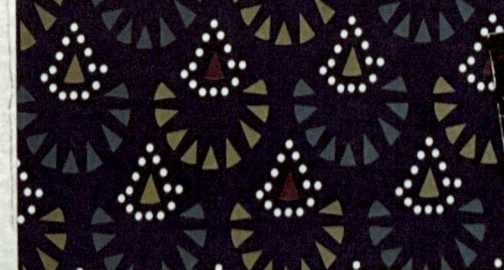

Part of front entrance - Biltmore 4/25/22

Barbara

Lookin' on up!

BILTMORE

Group Late Afternoon Guided Tour

Late Afternoon Guided Tour
Upgrade to a
Biltmore Annual Pass today!

Mon, Apr
9:30AM
Group Ad

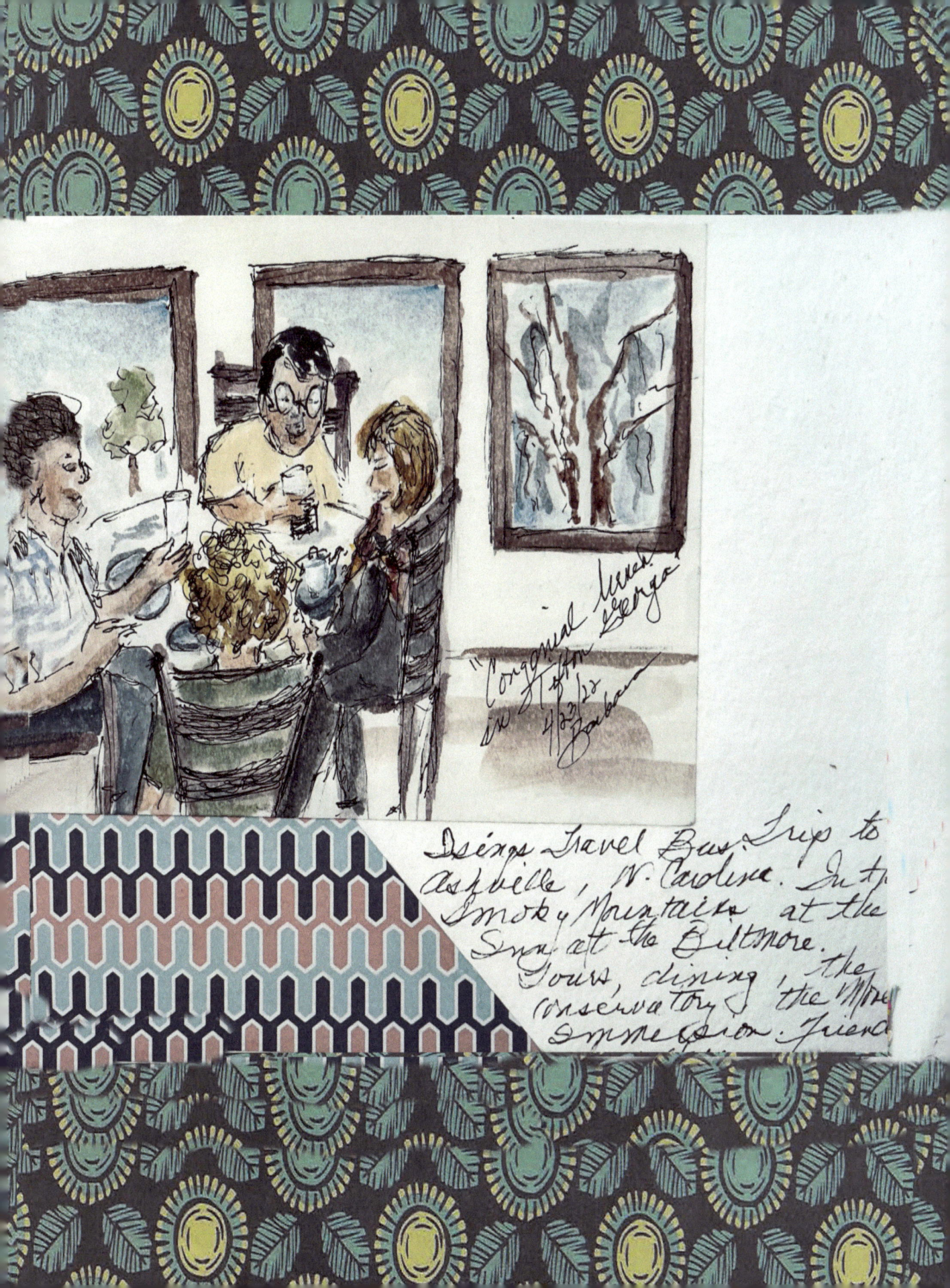

"Congenial Meal
in Tappan, Georgia"
4/23/22
Barbara

Isings Travel Bus Trip to
Ashville, N. Carolina. Into
Smoky Mountains at the
Snug at the Biltmore.
Tours, dining, the
conservatory, the "More
Impression. Friend

A Promise

Interrupted flight
Her pause to scan the meadow
Her choice the way ahead
As air beneath her wings
Fulfills an ancient promise

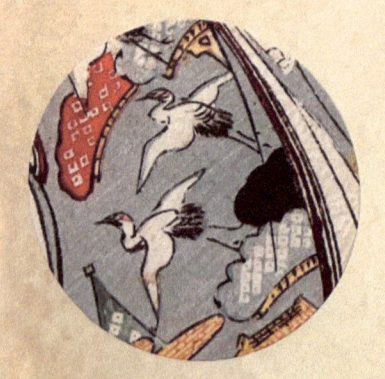

A Tanka
By Barbara Schmitz
September 1, 2022

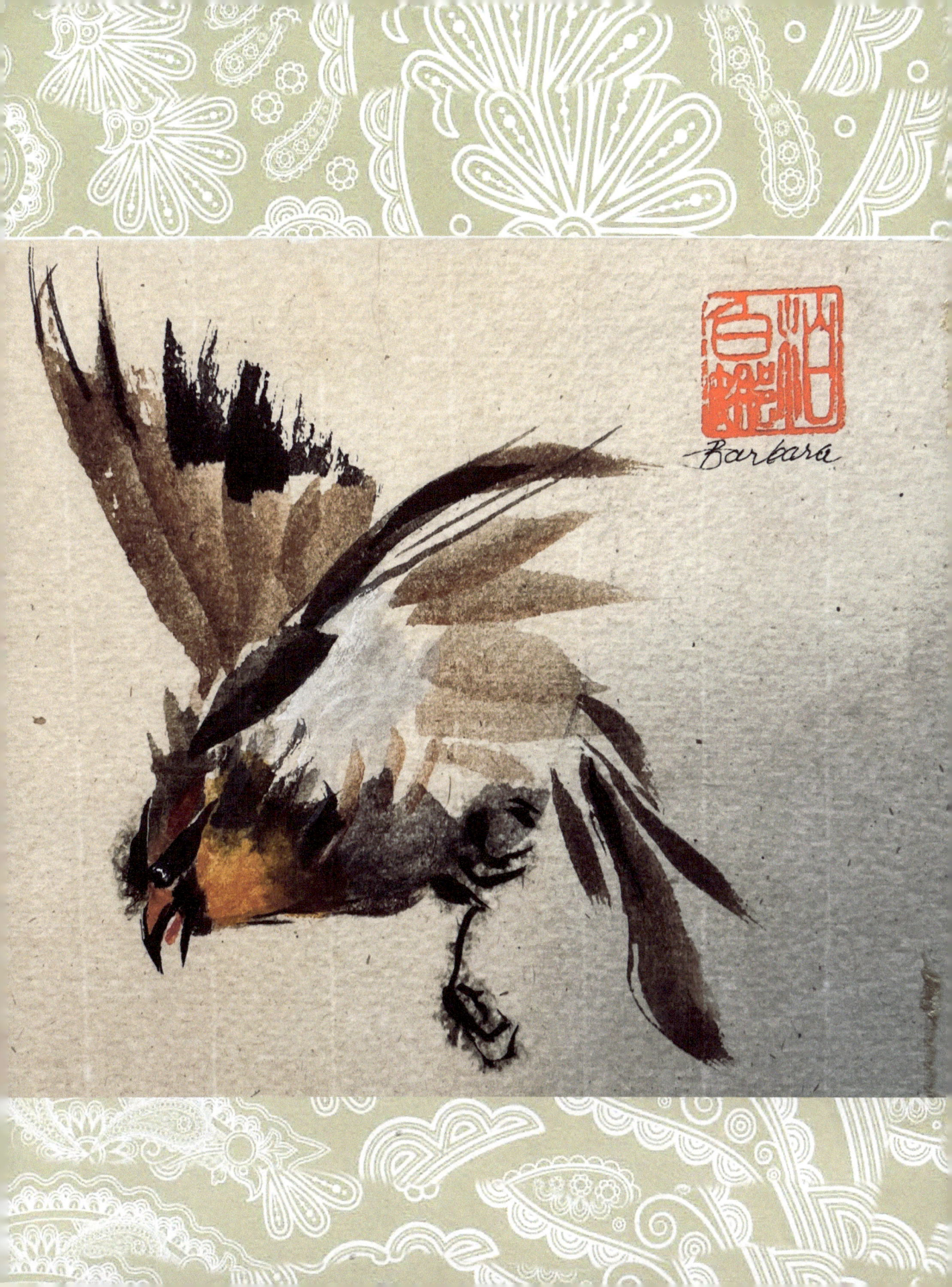

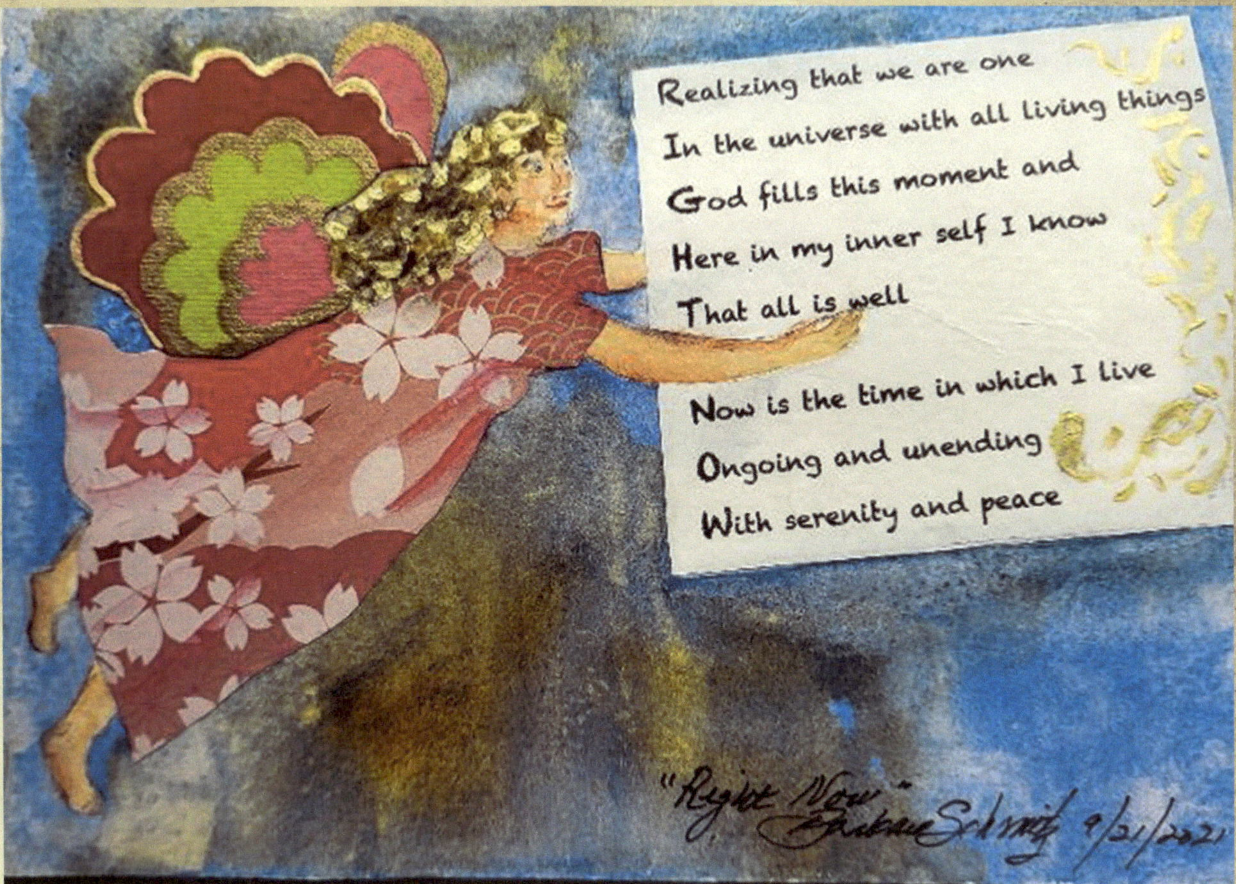

Realizing that we are one
In the universe with all living things
God fills this moment and
Here in my inner self I know
That all is well

Now is the time in which I live
Ongoing and unending
With serenity and peace

"Right Now"
Barbara Schmidt 9/31/2021

~The End~

www.ingramcontent.com/pod-product-compliance
Lightning Source LLC
Chambersburg PA
CBHW041519280526
45792CB00004B/1309